M. (Moses) Mielziner

A Selection from the Book of Psalms for School and Family

use

M. (Moses) Mielziner

A Selection from the Book of Psalms for School and Family use

ISBN/EAN: 9783744768320

Printed in Europe, USA, Canada, Australia, Japan

Cover: Foto ©Lupo / pixelio.de

More available books at **www.hansebooks.com**

A SELECTION

FROM

THE BOOK OF PSALMS,

FOR

SCHOOL AND FAMILY USE.

ARRANGED

BY

REV. DR. M. MIELZINER.

Published by
The Hebrew Sabbath-School Union of America.

1888.
FROM THE AMERICAN HEBREW PRINTING HOUSE,
THE BLOCH PUBLISHING AND PRINTING COMPANY,
CINCINNATI, O.

INTRODUCTION.

The Book of Psalms, also called the Psalter, forms a part of the Sacred Scripture, and contains a collection of 150 religious and devotional poems, composed by sacred bards belonging to different periods of Israel's ancient history. The Hebrew name of this collection is *Tehillim*, the book of *hymns*, or *songs of praise*. This appellation, however, applies to a part only of the songs contained in this book, as many of them belong to a different character of religious poetry. The word Psalm, derived from a Greek word meaning to play on a stringed instrument, is the translation of the Hebrew *Mizmor*, which is found in the heading of fifty-six psalms, and signifies a song to be accompanied by a musical instrument.

In our Hebrew Bible the Book of Psalms is divided into five great divisions, or books, corresponding to the five divisions of the Pentateuch. The first book contains forty-one psalms; the second thirty-one (xlii.-lxxii.); the third seventeen (lxxiii.-lxxxix.); the fourth seventeen (xc.-cvi.); and the fifth forty-four psalms (cvii.-cl.). Each closing psalm in these divisions ends with a special doxology (praise to God); the first three with a double *Amen* and the last two with *Hallelujah.*

The five divisions appear to represent five successive compilations of the psalms. This is evident from the circumstance that to the closing psalm of the second book the words are added: "The prayers of David, the son of Jesse, are ended." This statement shows that the compiler supposed that no more psalms of David were extant, although the following three books contain eighteen other psalms, which, according to their headings, are ascribed to that royal bard. When and by whom the single compilations of the psalms and their final collection into one book have been made, can not be stated.

CLASSIFICATION OF THE PSALMS.

Some of the Psalms were spontaneous effusions of the poetic mind and heart, occasioned by reflections on personal or national circumstances; others were composed for the express purpose of being used at the public worship in the temple.

In regard to their contents, the Psalms may be divided into:

1. *Hymns* in praise of God, glorifying Him either generally as God of nature and of man (f. ex., Ps. viii.; civ.; cxlv.); or as God of nature and the protector, deliverer and law-giver of Israel (f. ex., Ps. xxix.; xxxiii.; cxlvii.; cxlviii.).

2. *Prayers* for Divine help and protection under personal or national afflictions, or for merciful forgiveness of sins (f. ex., Ps. vi.; xvii.; xxxviii.; li.; lxxxvi.; cxxx.).

3. *Psalms of Thanksgiving* for deliverance from distress or for Divine mercies in general (f. ex., Ps. xxx.; xxxiv.; xlvi.; cxvi.).

4. *Religious Songs* in general, as odes to God and reflections on his Divine attributes (Ps. xc.; cxxxix.); expressions of religious sentiments and convictions, confidence, hope, submission (Ps. xxiii.; xxvii.; xci.; cxxi.); longing for the worship of God in his temple (Ps. xlii.; lxxxiv,).

5. *Didactic Poems* on the condition of the pious and the godless (Ps. i.; xxxvii.; xlix.; lxxiii.; cxii.); on the true mode of serving God (Ps. l.); on the way to forgiveness of sins (Ps. xxxii.).

6. *Historical and National Psalms*, containing allusions to certain events in the ancient history of Israel and to the Divine guidance manifested therein, as well as to the warnings and admonitions to be derived therefrom (Ps. lxxviii.; lxxxi.; lxxxv.; cxiv.; cxxvi.; cxxix.). Hereto may be added also those Psalms which have special allusions to certain Kings of Israel (Ps. ii.; xx.; xlv.; lxxii.); or to Jerusalem and Zion (xlviii.; lxxxvii.; cxxii.; cxxxii.).

TITLES OF THE PSALMS.

Most of the Psalms are, in the Bible, provided with a title or inscription, which in general indicates the author to whom that Psalm is ascribed; in some instances also the supposed occasion on which it was composed, as, f. e., Ps. v., " A Psalm of David, when he fled from his son Absalom." In some Psalms such a title is preceded by " For the Chief Musician," indicating that this Psalm was committed to the chief of the temple singers, to set it to appropriate music. Sometimes the title designates also the character of the Psalm, the style of its poetry, or the instrument with which it was to be accompanied, or the tune which was to be sung, as in Ps. viii., " For the Chief Musician; on the Gittith; a Psalm of David; " or in Ps. xlvi., " For the Chief Musician; of the sons of Korah; set to Alamoth; a Song."

These titles, though undoubtedly of great antiquity, are not supposed to have been prefixed by the authors themselves, but rather by the compilers.* Only thirty-four Psalms are without titles.

AUTHORS OF THE PSALMS.

In the inscriptions just mentioned the following authors of Psalms are named:

1. *Moses*, as the author of Ps. xc. only.
2. *David*, as author of seventy-three Psalms.
3. *Solomon*, to whom two Psalms (lxxii. and cxxvii.) are ascribed.
4. *Asaph*, who was a poet and Chief of Choirs in the time of David, is mentioned as author of twelve Psalms (l. and lxxiii.-lxxxiii.). Some of these Psalms, however, belong probably to his descendants, who were temple singers in the time of Ezra.
5. *The Sons of Korah*, a Levitical family of singers, to whom eleven Psalms are ascribed (xlii.-xlix.; lxxxiv.; lxxxv.; lxxxvii.).
6. *Heman*, the Ezrahite, whose name occurs in the title of only one Psalm (lxxxviii.), in connection with the singer family of the Sons of Korah.
7. *Ethan*, the Ezrahite, probably belonging to the same family, is mentioned as author of one Psalm (lxxxix.).

---

* As it is very difficult to explain the meaning of many of these titles, especially those referring to the musical performance, and, as they are not at all necessary for the understanding of the Psalms to which they are prefixed, we have omitted them in the present " Selections from the Book of Psalms," and retained only the titles referring to the traditional authors.

In this connection it may also be proper to state that the heading printed in *Italics* over each Psalm in this collection, and indicating its general contents, are not found in the Hebrew Bible, and have been added by us, according to the best commentaries.

: From the above it will be seen that the authorship of the greatest number of those Psalms which bear a title is credited to *David*. There can be no doubt that this royal bard, who elsewhere in Scripture is called the *Sweet Psalmist of Israel*, did compose most of the Psalms ascribed to him, and perhaps also some of those which have no titles. But several titles of Psalms bearing the name of David, or of Solomon and Asaph, can not well be authentic, since those Psalms contain allusions to events and circumstances belonging to a later period of Jewish history. The authors of those and of the anonymous Psalms can not be ascertained. Some of them evidently belonged to the period of the Kings after David, some to that of the Babylonian captivity, and some to the time after the return from that captivity.

POETIC FORM OF THE PSALMS.

All the Psalms giving expression to emotions and aspirations of the heart are composed in poetic language which is characterized by the frequent use of figures, similes, metaphors and personifications. In regard to the form of verses, the poetry of the Psalms, like ancient Hebrew poetry in general, has no rhyme, nor a meter of long and short syllables, but instead of both it has a peculiar feature which is called *parallelism*. It consists in this, that a verse is divided into parts or lines, generally two, but sometimes three or four, and these lines, containing in the original almost an equal number of words, correspond to each other in different ways, so that either one line, with slight modifications, expresses the same sentiment as the other, or it expresses something in contrast with the other, or the second line completes or continues the thought of the former. The following examples may illustrate this:

> "The heavens declare the glory of God,
> And the firmament showeth his handiwork."

Here the second line is almost identical in meaning with the first.

> "In the morning it flourisheth and shooteth up,
> And in the evening it is cut down and withered."

Here the second line forms a contrast with the first.

Of the different ways in which the two lines complete each other, one example may be given in which one line contains a simile to the thought expressed in the other:

> "As the hart panteth after the water brook,
> So panteth my soul after Thee, O God."

The same correspondence as between two lines is also found when the verse is divided into three or four lines, as:

> "A thousand shall fall by thy side,
> And ten thousand at thy right hand;
> But Thee it shall not touch."

Here the first two lines are synonymous, while the third forms a contrast to both of them. Or:

> "Though a host should encamp against me,
> My heart shall not fear;
> Though war should rise against me,
> Even then will I be confident."

In this four-line verse the first line corresponds with the third, and the second with the fourth, while the second forms a contrast to the first and the fourth to the third.

By this parallelism, which admits of a great variety of combinations, Hebrew poetry has a peculiar rhythm, not of measured feet and syllables, but a rhythm of thought and sentiment.

VALUE OF THE PSALMS.

Even if viewed simply as poetical productions, the Psalms have a great value as remnants of the lyric poetry of Hebrew antiquity. Some of these Psalms are so sublime in their sentiment and so full of beauty and charm in their expressions as to be deservedly counted among the most precious gems of all human poetry.

But the principal value of the Psalms arises from their exquisite adaptation to the devotional purposes of the individual as well as the congregational worship of the Supreme Being. The emotions and experiences which prompted the sacred bards of ancient Israel to sing these Psalms are still the emotions and experiences of every pious heart. How varied are the feelings to which these Psalms give expression! Sorrow, grief, fear, remorse, penitence, hope, confidence,

gratitude, love, joy, admiration—whatever moves and elevates and
soothes the human heart is expressed in them. It has been properly
remarked that there is scarcely a circumstance in human life in which
one may not repair to the Psalms and find in them something appropriate to his situation and to his frame of mind.

It is therefore that the Book of Psalms has become so endeared to
religious hearts in all generations, and that so many of those songs
which more than two or three thousand years ago came from the sacred
lyre of Israel's bards and resounded in the temple of Jerusalem,
still, until this day, hold their place in the devotional services, not
only of our synagogues and temples, but also of the different denomina-
tions of the Church.

To make our rising generation acquainted with a choice selection
from these precious songs is the object of the present little volume,
which is published under the auspices of the Hebrew Sabbath School
Union of America.   DR. M. MIELZINER.

THE PSALMS.

1.   *PSALM I.*

The happiness of the righteous and the doom of the wicked.

1 HAPPY is the man who walketh not in the counsel of the
   wicked,
   Nor standeth in the way of sinners,
   Nor sitteth in the seat of scoffers;
2 But whose delight is in the law of the LORD;
   And in his law he meditateth day and night.
3 He shall be like a tree planted by the streams of water,
   That bringeth forth its fruit in its season,
   Whose leaf also doth not wither:
   And all that he doeth shall prosper.
4 Not so the wicked;
   But they are like the chaff which the wind driveth away.
5 Therefore the wicked shall not stand in the judgment,
   Nor sinners in the congregation of the righteous.
6 For the LORD knoweth the way of the righteous;
   But the way of the wicked leadeth to ruin.

2.   *PSALM VIII.*

The glory of God and the dignity of man.

A Psalm of David.

1 Eternal God, our Lord!
   How excellent is thy name in all the earth!
   Thou who hast set thy glory above the heavens.

2 Out of the mouth of children and sucklings hast thou
    founded a power,
  Because of thine adversaries,
  To silence the enemy and the revengeful.*

3 When I consider the heavens, the work of thy fingers,
  The moon and the stars which thou hast ordained :—
4 What is man that thou art mindful of him,
  And the son of man that thou carest for him?
5 Yet thou hast made him a little less than divine,
  And hast crowned him with glory and honor.
6 Thou hast given him dominion over the works of thy hands;
  Thou hast put all things under his feet :—
7 All sheep and oxen,
  Yea, and the beasts of the field ;
8 The fowl of the air and the fish of the sea,
  Whatsoever passeth through the paths of the seas.

9 Eternal God, our Lord,
  How excellent is thy name in all the earth !

3.   *PSALM XV.*

              The qualifications of a true worshiper.

                     A Psalm of David.

1 LORD, who shall sojourn in thy tabernacle?
  Who shall dwell upon thy holy hill?

2 He that walketh uprightly, and doeth righteousness,
  And speaketh truth in his heart.

---

* The meaning of this verse appears to be that every coming generation (" children and sucklings ") will be impressed by the greatness and beauty of God's world
and always anew bear witness to the power and glory of the Creator, thus silencing
his " adversaries " and " enemies "—namely, those who deny God.

3 He that slandereth not with his tongue,
  Nor doeth injury to his neighbor,
  Nor uttereth a reproach against his friend.
4 In whose eyes a vile person is despised;
  But who honoreth them that fear the LORD.
  He that sweareth to his own hurt, and changeth not.
5 He that lendeth not his money for usury,
  Nor taketh a bribe against the innocent.
  He that doeth these things shall never be moved.

4.   *PSALM XVI.*

*Reliance upon God alone; satisfaction with his blessings and rejoicing hope
of future protection and favor.*

A Psalm of David.

1 Preserve me, O God! for in thee do I put my trust.
2 I have said unto the LORD, thou art my Lord;
  I have no happiness beyond thee!
3 The holy that are in the land,—
  They are the excellent in whom is all my delight.
4 They who hasten after other gods have many sorrows;
  Their drink-offerings of blood will I not offer,
  Nor take their names upon my lips.
5 The LORD is the portion of mine inheritance and of my cup;
  Thou wilt maintain my lot!
6 The lines are fallen unto me in pleasant places;
  Yea, I have a goodly heritage.

7 I will bless the LORD, who hath given me counsel;
  Yea, my heart admonisheth me in the night.
8 I have set the LORD always before me;
  Because he is at my right hand, I shall not fall.
9 Therefore my heart is glad, and my spirit rejoiceth;
  My flesh also dwelleth in safety.

10 For thou wilt not give me up to the grave:
Nor wilt thou suffer thy pious servant to see destruction.
11 Thou wilt show me the path of life;
In thy presence is fullness of joy:
In thy right hand there are pleasures for evermore.

5.   *PSALM XIX.*

*The glory of God manifested in the creation, and in the law given to man.
Prayer for forgiveness and deliverance from temptation.*

A Psalm of David.

1 The heavens declare the glory of God;
And the firmament showeth his handiwork.
2 Day unto day uttereth speech,
And night unto night showeth knowledge.
3 There is no speech nor language;
Their voice can not be heard.
4 Yet their sound goeth forth to all the earth.
And their words to the end of the world.
In them hath he set a tabernacle for the sun,
5 Which cometh forth like a bridegroom from his chamber,
And rejoiceth, like a strong man, to run his course.
6 His going forth is from the end of the heaven,
And his circuit unto the ends of it:
And there is nothing hid from his heat.

7 The law of the LORD is perfect, reviving the soul:
The testimony of the LORD is sure, making wise the simple.
8 The precepts of the LORD are right, rejoicing the heart:
The commandment of the LORD is pure, enlightening the
eyes.
9 The fear of the LORD is clean, enduring forever:
The judgments of the LORD are true, and righteous alto
gether.

10 More to be desired are they than gold, yea, than much fine
   gold :
   Sweeter also than honey and the honeycomb.
11 Moreover by them is thy servant warned :
   In keeping of them there is great reward.

12 Who can discern his errors?
   Clear thou me from hidden faults !
13 Keep back thy servant also from presumptuous sins ;
   Let them not have dominion over me : then shall I be
   perfect,
   And I shall be clear from great transgression.
14 May the words of my mouth and the meditation of my
   ⋅ heart be acceptable in thy sight,
   O LORD, my rock, and my redeemer !

6.   *PSALM XXIII.*

Confidence in God's graceful care and protection.

A Psalm of David.

1 The LORD is my shepherd ; I shall not want.
2 He maketh me to lie down in green pastures :
   He leadeth me beside the still waters.
3 He reviveth my soul :
   He guideth me in the paths of righteousness for his name's
   sake.
4 Yea, though I walk through the valley of the shadow of
   death,
   I will fear no evil ; for thou art with me :
   Thy rod and thy staff they comfort me.
5 Thou preparest a table before me in the presence of mine
   enemies :
   Thou hast anointed my head with oil ; my cup runneth over.

6 Surely goodness and mercy shall follow me all the days of
    my life :
And I will dwell in the house of the LORD forever.

7.   *PSALM XXIV.*

Hymn, on the occasion of introducing the ark of covenant into the sanctuary.

A Psalm of David

1 The earth is the LORD's, and the fullness thereof;
    The world, and they that dwell therein.
2 For he hath founded it upon the seas,
    And established it upon the floods.
3 Who shall ascend the hill of the LORD?
    And who shall stand in his holy plac·?
4 He that hath clean hands, and a pure heart;
    Who hath not lifted up his soul unto vanity,
    And hath not sworn deceitfully.
5 He shall receive a blessing from the LORD,
    And righteousness from the God of his salvation.
6 This is the generation of them that seek him,
    That seek thy face, O God of Jacob!   [Selah.*]

7 Lift up your heads, O ye gates ;
    And be·ye lift up, ye everlasting doors :
    And the King of glory shall come in!
8 " Who is this King of glory? "
    The LORD strong and mighty,
    The ·LORD mighty in battle.

9 Lift up your heads, O ye gates ;
    Yea, lift them up, ye everlasting doors:
    And·the King of glory shall come !
10 " Who is this King of glory? "
    The LORD of hosts,
    He is the King of glory.   [Selah.]

*The word Selah occurring in this and in many other Psalms is Hebrew, and
supposed to be a sign denoting a pause, or a change of tune in the musical performance of the song.

8. *PSALM XXVII.*

At a time of distress, the psalmist expresses his confidence in God, and his desire for his temple. He then prays for relief in his desolate condition and trusts that he shall obtain it.

Of David.

1 The LORD is my light and my salvation;
whom shall I fear?
The LORD is the strength of my life;
of whom shall I be afraid?
2 When evil-doers came upon me to devour me,
Even mine adversaries and my foes,
they stumbled and fell.
3 Though a host should encamp against me,
my heart shall not fear;
Though war should rise against me,
even then will I be confident.
4 One thing have I asked of the LORD,
that do I desire:
That I may dwell in the house of the LORD
all the days of my life,
To behold the grace of the LORD,
and to inquire in his temple.
5 For he shall hide me in his pavilion
on the day of trouble.
In the shelter of his tabernacle shall he conceal me;
upon a rock shall he lift me up.
6 And now shall my head be lifted up
above mine enemies round about me,
And I will offer in his tabernacle sacrifices of joy;
I will sing and play the harp to the LORD.

7 Hear my voice, O LORD! when I cry unto thee;
Have mercy upon me, and answer me!
8 When thou saidst, Seek ye my face! my heart said unto thee:
Thy face, LORD, will I seek.

9 Hide not thy face from me;
Put not thy servant away in anger:
Thou hast been my help;
Cast me not off, neither forsake me, O God of my salvation !
10 For my father and my mother have forsaken me,
But the LORD will take me up.

11 Teach me thy way, O LORD !
And lead me in a plain path,
Because of mine enemies !
12 Deliver me not over unto the will of mine adversaries !
For false witnesses are risen up against me, and such as
breathe out cruelty.

13 I had fainted, unless I had believed to see the goodness of
the LORD
In the land of the living.
14 Hope thou in the LORD !
Be strong, and let thy heart take courage;
Yea, hope thou in the LORD !

9.   *PSALM XXIX.*

The glory of God, as manifested in a thunder-storm.

A Psalm of David.

1 Give unto the LORD, O ye sons of the mighty !
Give unto the LORD glory and strength !
2 Give unto the LORD the glory due unto his name;
Worship the LORD in the beauty of holiness !

3 The voice of the LORD is heard above the waters:
The God of glory thundereth—
Even the LORD above the great waters.
4 The voice of the LORD is powerful;
The voice of the LORD is full of majesty.

5 The voice of the LORD breaketh the cedars ;
Yea, the LORD breaketh in pieces the cedars of Lebanon.
6 He maketh them also to skip like a calf;
Lebanon and Sirion like a young buffalo.
7 The voice of the LORD cleaveth the flames of fire.
8 The voice of the LORD shaketh the wilderness ;
The LORD shaketh the wilderness of Kadesh.
9 The voice of the LORD causeth the hinds to start,
And strippeth the forests bare ;—
While, in his temple, everything saith, Glory !

10 The LORD sat as King at the Flood ;
Yea, the LORD sitteth as King forever.
11 The LORD will give strength unto his people ;
The LORD will bless his people with peace.

10. *PSALM XXX.*

Thanksgiving for deliverance from distress.

A Psalm of David.

1 I will extol thee, O LORD ! for thou hast lifted me up,
And hast not suffered my foes to rejoice over me.
2 O LORD, my God !
I cried unto thee, and thou hast healed me.
3 O LORD ! thou hast raised me up from the underworld ;
Thou hast kept me alive, that I should not go down to the
pit.
4 Sing praise unto the LORD, O ye his pious servants,
And give thanks to his holy name !
5 For his anger is but for a moment;
But his favor through life ;
In the evening weeping may come to stay for a night,
But in the morning there is a shout of joy.
6 As for me, I said in my prosperity,
" I shall never be moved ! "

7 Thou, O Lord! by thy favor hadst made my mountain to
stand strong;
Thou didst hide thy face, and I was troubled.
8 I cried to thee, O Lord!
And unto the Lord I made supplication:
9 "What profit is there in my blood, when I go down to the pit?
Shall the dust praise thee? shall it declare thy truth?
10 Hear, O Lord, and have mercy upon me!
Lord! be thou my helper!"
11 Thou hast turned for me my mourning into dancing;
Thou hast loosed my sackcloth, and girded me with gladness:
12 That my soul may sing praise to thee, and not be silent.
O Lord, my God! I will give thanks unto thee forever!

11. *PSALM XXXII.*

The happiness of him whose sins are forgiven.

A Meditation of David.

1 Happy is he whose transgression is forgiven,
whose sin is covered.
2 Happy is the man unto whom the Lord imputeth not in-
iquity,
And in whose spirit there is no guile.
3 When I kept silence, my bones waxed old
Through my groaning all the day long.
4 For day and night thy hand was heavy upon me;
My moisture was changed as in the drought of summer.
[Selah.]
5 I acknowledged my sin unto thee, and mine iniquity have
I not hid:
I said, "I will confess my transgressions unto the Lord;"
And thou forgavest the iniquity of my sin. [Selah.]

6 For this let every pious man pray unto thee in a time when
  thou mayest be found;
  Surely when the great waters overflow they shall not reach
  unto him.
7 Thou art my hiding place; thou wilt preserve me from
  trouble;
  Thou wilt compass me about with songs of deliverance.

[Selah.]

8 I will instruct thee and teach thee in the way which thou
  shalt go;
  I will counsel thee with mine eye upon thee.
9 Be ye not as the horse, or as the mule, which have no understanding:
  Whose trappings must be bit and bridle to hold them in,
  Else they will not come near unto thee.
10 Many are the sorrows of the wicked;
  But he that trusteth in the LORD, mercy shall compass him
  about.
11 Be glad in the LORD, and rejoice, ye righteous:
  And shout for joy, all ye that are upright in heart!

12. *PSALM XXXIII.*

*A hymn to God as the creator and governor of the world, and the pro-
tector of his people.*

1 Rejoice in the LORD, O ye righteous!
  Praise is comely for the upright.
2 Give thanks unto the LORD with the harp,
  Sing praises unto him with the ten-stringed psaltery!
3 Sing unto him a new song;
  Play skillfully with a loud noise!

4 For the word of the LORD is right;
  And all his work is done in faithfulness.

5 He loveth righteousness and justice;
 The earth is full of the loving kindness of the LORD.
6 By the word of the LORD were the heavens made;
 And all the host of them by the breath of his mouth.
7 He gathereth the waters of the sea together as an heap;
 He layeth up the deeps in storehouses.

8 Let all the earth fear the LORD;
 Let all the inhabitants of the world stand in awe of him.
9 For he spake, and it was done;
 He commanded, and it stood fast.

10 The LORD bringeth the counsel of the nations to naught;
 He maketh the thoughts of the peoples to be of none effect.
11 The counsel of the LORD standeth fast for ever,
 The thoughts of his heart, to all generations.

12 Happy is the nation whose God is the LORD;
 The people whom he hath chosen for his own inheritance.
13 The LORD looketh from heaven;
 He beholdeth all the sons of men.
14 From the place of his habitation he looketh forth
 Upon all the inhabitants of the earth;
15 He who formed the hearts of them all,
 He observeth all their works.

16 There is no king saved by the multitude of his forces,
 A mighty man is not delivered by great strength.
17 The horse is a vain thing for safety,
 Neither shall he deliver any by his great power.

18 Behold, the eye of the LORD is upon them that fear him,
 Upon them that trust in his mercy;
19 To deliver their soul from death,
 And to keep them alive in famine.

20 Our soul hath waited for the LORD;
 He is our help and our shield.

21 For our heart shall rejoice in him,
 Because we have trusted in his holy name.
22 Let then thy mercy, O Lord! be upon us,
 According as we hope in thee!

13. *PSALM XXXIV.*

Thanksgiving for deliverance from distress, and a description of the happiness of the good and the misery of the wicked.

A Psalm of David.

1 I will bless the Lord at all times;
 His praise shall continually be in my mouth.
2 My soul shall make her boast in the Lord;
 The afflicted shall hear thereof, and be glad.
3 O magnify the Lord with me,
 And let us exalt his name together!

4 I sought the Lord, and he answered me,
 And delivered me from all my fears.
5 They who look up to him, shall have light;
 And their faces shall never be ashamed.
6 This afflicted man cried, and the Lord heard him.
 And saved him out of all his troubles.
7 The angel of the Lord encampeth round about them that
 fear him,
 And delivereth them.
8 O taste, and see that the Lord is good,
 Happy is the man that trusteth in him!
9 O fear the Lord, ye his saints!
 For there is no want to them that fear him.
10 The young lions do lack, and suffer hunger;
 But they that seek the Lord shall not want any good thing.

11 Come, ye children, hearken unto me!
 I will teach you the fear of the Lord.

12 Who is he that desireth life,
   And loveth many days, in which he may see good?
13 Keep thy tongue from evil,
   And thy lips from speaking guile !
14 Depart from evil, and do good ;
   Seek peace, and pursue it !

15 The eyes of the LORD are toward the righteous,
   And his ears are open unto their cry.
16 The face of the LORD is against them that do evil,
   To cut off their remembrance from the earth.
17 The righteous cry, and the LORD heareth,
   And delivereth them from all their troubles.
18 The LORD is nigh unto them that are of a broken heart,
   And saveth such as be of a contrite spirit.
19 Many are the afflictions of the righteous ;
   But the LORD delivereth him from them all.
20 He keepeth all his bones ;
   Not one of them is broken.
21 Evil destroyeth the wicked,
   And they that hate the righteous suffer for it.
22 The LORD redeemeth the soul of his servants,
   And none of them that trust in him shall suffer.

14.   *PART OF PSALM XXXVI.*

v. 6–13.

Praising the goodness of God, and praying for his help.

1 Thy loving-kindness, O Lord ! reaches to the heavens ;
  Thy faithfulness unto the skies.
2 Thy righteousness is like the high mountains ;
  Thy judgments are a great deep ;
  O LORD ! thou preservest man and beast.
3 How precious is thy loving-kindness, O God !
  And the children of men take refuge under the shadow of
     thy wings.

4 They shall be satisfied with the abundance of thy house ;
  And thou shalt. make them drink of the full stream of thy
    pleasures.
5 For with thee is the fountain of life ;
  Through thy light we see light.
6 O continue thy loving-kindness unto them that know thee ;
  And thy righteousness to the upright in heart.
7 Let not the foot of pride come against me,
  Nor the hand of the wicked drive me away.
8 Lo! already are the workers of iniquity fallen ;
  They are thrust down, and are unable to rise !

15.   *PARTS OF PSALM XXXVII.*

(vs. 1-6; 23-24; 35-37.)

*A Didactic Poem on the final reward of the righteous and the
punishment of the wicked.*

Of David.

1 Be not thou angry on the account of wicked,
  Nor be envious of those who do iniquity.
2 For they shall soon be cut down like the grass,
  And wither as the green herb.
3 Trust in the LORD, and do good ;
  Abide in the land, and follow after faithfulness.
4 Delight thyself also in the LORD ;
  And he shall give thee the desires of thine heart.
5 Commit thy way unto the LORD ;
  Trust in him, and he will give thee success.
6 He will cause thy righteousness to shine forth like the light,
  And thy justice like the noonday's brightness.

*   *   *   *   *   *   *   *   *

7 The steps of the good man are established by the LORD ;
  And he delighteth in his way.
8 Though he fall. he shall not be utterly cast down,
  For the LORD upholdeth his hand.

9 I have been young, and now am old;
Yet have I not seen the righteous forsaken,
Nor his offspring begging their bread.
10 He is ever merciful, and lendeth;
And his offspring shall be blessed.
11 Depart from evil, and do good,
And dwell for evermore.
12 For the LORD loveth judgment,
And forsaketh not his pious servants.
13 They are preserved forever;
But the seed of the wicked shall be cut off.

*   *   *   *   *   *   *   *   *

14 I have seen the wicked in great power,
And spreading himself like a green tree in its native soil.
15 But he passed away, and, lo! he was no more;
Yea, I sought him, but he could not be found.
16 Mark the perfect man and behold the upright:
For the latter end of that man is peace.

16.   *PSALM XLII.*

*An afflicted exile expresses his aspiration after the temple and worship
of God.*

A Song of the Sons of Korah.

1 As the hart panteth after the water brooks,
So panteth my soul after thee, O God!
2 My soul thirsteth for God, for the living God:
When shall I come to appear before God?
3 My tears have been my food day and night,
While they continually say unto me, "Where is thy God?"
4 When I think of it, I pour out my soul in grief,
How I once walked with the multitude,
Walked slowly with them to the house of God,
Amid sounds of joy and praise, with the festive multitude!

5 Why art thou cast down, O my soul?
And why art thou disquieted within me?
Hope thou in God : for I shall yet praise him
For the help of his countenance !

6 O my God! my soul is cast down within me :
Therefore do I remember thee from the land of Jordan,
And from the summits of Hermon, from the low mount,*

7 Deep calleth unto deep at the noise of thy waterfalls ;
All thy waves and thy billows have gone over me !

8 Yet the LORD will command his loving-kindness in the day-
time,
And in the night his song shall be with me,
Even a prayer unto the God of my life.

9 Now I say unto God, my rock, Why hast thou forgotten me?
Why go I mourning because of the oppression of the
enemy?

10 As with crushing in my bones, mine adversaries reproach
me ;
While they continually say unto me, " Where is thy God?'

11 Why art thou cast down, O my soul?
And why art thou disquieted within me?
Hope thou in God : for I shall yet praise him,
Who is the help of my countenance, and my God !

17.   *PSALM XLIII.*

Continuation of the preceding Song.

1 Judge me, O God ! and defend my cause against an ungodly
nation !
O deliver me from deceitful and unjust men !

---

*Hermon is a mountain on the northeastern border of Palestine. One of the lower mounts in the Hermon range was evidently the locality where the exiled poet just sojourned. From this place he looks longingly toward his home, and just as there in a strange land, the wild waters of the mountains roar around him, there seems to be a corresponding tumult in his soul, which the following verse describes

2 For thou art the God of my strength; why hast thou cast
    me off?
  Why go I mourning because of the oppression of the
    enemy?
3 O send out thy light and thy truth; let them lead me:
  Let them bring me unto thy holy hill,
  And to thy dwelling place!
4 Then will I go unto the altar of God,   ·
  Unto God, my exceeding joy:
  And upon the harp will I praise thee, O God, my God!

5 Why art thou cast down, O my soul?
  And why art thou disquieted within me?
  Hope thou in God: for I shall yet praise him,
  Who is the help of my countenance, and my God!

18.   *PSALM XLVI.*

*Thanksgiving for victory over enemies, and trust in God as a refuge and
defense of his people.*

A Song of the Sons of Korah.

1 God is our refuge and strength,
  An ever-present help in trouble.
2 Therefore will we not fear, though the earth do change,
  And though the mountains tremble in the heart of the seas;
3 Though its waters roar and be troubled,
  Though the mountains shake with the swelling thereof.
                                              [Selah.]

4 There is a river, the streams whereof make glad the city of
    God,
  The holy dwelling place of the Most High.
5 God is in the midst of her; she shall not be moved:
  God shall help her, and that right early.
6 The nations raged; kingdoms were moved:
  He uttered his voice, the earth melted.

7 The LORD of hosts is with us;
  The God of Jacob is our refuge.   [Selah.]

8 Come, behold the works of the LORD,
  What desolations he hath made in the earth!
9 He maketh wars to cease unto the end of the earth;
  He breaketh the bow, and cutteth the spear asunder;
  He burneth the chariots in the fire.

10 "Desist, and know that I am God:
   I will be exalted among the nations, I will be exalted
      throughout the earth!"
11 The LORD of hosts is with us;
   The God of Jacob is our refuge.   [Selah.]

19.   *PSALM XLIX.*

A didactic poem on the conditions of the righteous and the wicked.

A Psalm of the Sons of Korah.

1 Hear this, all ye peoples;
  Give ear, all ye inhabitants of the world:
2 Both low and high,
  Rich and poor together.
3 My mouth shall speak wisdom;
  And the meditation of my heart shall be of understanding.
4 I will incline mine ear to a parable;
  I will open my dark saying upon the harp.

5 Wherefore should I fear in the days of evil,
  When the iniquity of my adversaries encompasseth me?
6 They that trust in their wealth,
  And glory in the multitude of their riches;
7 None of them can by any means redeem his brother,
  Nor give to God a ransom for him;
8 (For the redemption of their life is too costly,
  And must be let alone forever:)

9 That he should still live alway,
That he should not see the pit.

10 For he seeth that wise men die,
The fool and the brutish alike perish,
And leave their wealth to others.

11 They imagine, that their houses will endure forever,
And their dwelling-places to all generations;
They call their lands after their own names.

12 But man being in honor abideth not;
He is like the beasts that perish.

13 This their way is their folly;
Yet after them men approve their sayings.   [Selah.]

14 Like sheep they are cast into the underworld;
Death shall feed upon them;
And the upright shall have dominion over them in the
morning;
Their form shall be consumed in the underworld, and there
shall be no habitation for it.

15 But God will redeem my soul from the underworld;
For he shall receive me.   [Selah]

16 Be not thou afraid when one is made rich,
When the glory of his house is increased:

17 For when he dieth he shall carry nothing away;
His glory shall not descend after him.

18 Though while he lived he blest his soul,
And men praise thee when thou doest well to thyself,

19 It shall go to the generation of his fathers,
Who never more shall see the light

20 Man that is in honor, but understandeth not,
Is like the beasts that perish.

20.   *PSALM L.*

A didactic poem on the true mode of serving God.

A Psalm of Asaph.

1 The mighty God, the Lord, speaketh, and calleth the
earth,
From the rising of the sun to its going down.

2 Out of Zion, the perfection of beauty,
  God shineth forth.
3 Our God is coming, and will not keep silence :
  A fire devoureth before him,
  And around him there rageth a mighty storm.
4 He calleth to the heavens above,
  And to the earth, to judge his people :
5 " Gather together unto me, my pious servants,
  Who have made a covenant with me by sacrifice ! "
6 (And the heavens shall declare his righteousness :
  For God is judge himself.)   [Selah.]

7 " Hear, O my people, and I will speak !
  O Israel, and I will testify against thee !
  I am God, even thy God.
8 I will not reprove thee for thy sacrifices ;
  For thy burnt-offerings are continually before me.
9 I will take no bullock out of thy house,
  Nor he-goats out of thy folds
10 For every beast of the forest is mine,
  And the cattle upon a thousand hills
11 I know all the fowls of the mountains,
  And the wild beasts of the fields are before me.
12 If I were hungry I would not tell thee,
  For the world is mine, and the fullness thereof.
13 Do I eat the flesh of bulls,
  Or drink the blood of goats?
14 Offer unto God thanksgiving,
  And pay thy vows unto the Most High !
15 Then call upon me in the day of trouble ;
  I will deliver thee, and thou shalt glorify me ! "

16 But unto the wicked God saith :
  " To what purpose dost thou talk of my statutes?
  And why bearest thou my covenant upon thy lips?
17 Thou who hatest instruction,
  And castest my words behind thee.

18 When thou seest a thief, thou art in friendship with him,
And hast fellowship with adulterers.
19 Thou lettest loose thy mouth to evil,
And thy tongue frameth deceit.
20 Thou sittest and speakest against thy brother;
Thou slanderest thine own mother's son.
21 These things hast thou done, and I kept silence;
Thou didst imagine that I was altogether like thyself;
But I will reprove thee, and set it in order before thine
eyes."

22 " Now consider this, ye that forget God,
Lest I tear in pieces, and there be none to deliver!
23 Whoso offereth thanksgiving honoreth me;
And to him who hath regard to his ways
Will I show the salvation of God."

21 *PSALM LI.*

A prayer of repentance.

A Psalm of David.

1 Be gracious unto me, O God! according to thy loving kind
ness;
According to the greatness of thy mercy, blot out my trans·
gressions!
2 Wash me thoroughly from mine iniquity,
And cleanse me from my sin!
3 For I acknowledge my transgressions,
And my sin is ever before me.
4 Against thee, thee only, have I sinned,
And done that which is evil in thy sight;
So that thou art just in thy sentence,
And righteous in thy judgment.

5 Behold! I was born in iniquity;
And in sin did my mother conceive me.

6 Behold! thou desirest truth in the inward parts ·
. So teach me wisdom in my inmost soul!
7 Purge me with hyssop, and I shall be clean;
Wash me, and I shall be whiter than snow!
8 Make me to hear joy and gladness,
That the bones which thou hast broken may rejoice!
9 Hide thy face from my sins,
And blot out all mine iniquities!

10 Create in me a clean heart, O God!
And renew a steadfast spirit within me!
11 Cast me not away from thy presence,
And take not thy holy spirit from me!
12 Restore unto me the joy of thy salvation,
And uphold me with a willing spirit!
13 Then will I teach transgressors thy ways;
And sinners shall return unto thee.
14 Deliver me from the guilt of blood, O God, thou God of my
salvation!
That my tongue may sing aloud of thy righteousness!

15 O LORD, open thou my lips,
That my mouth may show forth thy praise!
16 For thou delightest not in sacrifice; else would I give it;
. Thou hast no pleasure in burnt offering.
17 The sacrifices of God are a broken spirit:
A broken and a contrite heart, O God, thou wilt not
despise!

22 *PSALM LXV.*

*Praise is due to God for his grace. He governs all nature and mankind,
and blesses the earth with an abundant harvest.*

A Psalm of David. A Song.

1 Praise waiteth for thee, O God! in Zion:
And unto thee shall the vow be performed!
2 O thou that hearest prayer,
Unto thee shall all flesh come!

3 Iniquities prevail against me;
But thou wilt forgive our transgressions.
4 Happy is he whom thou choosest,
And bringest near thee to dwell in thy courts!
May we be satisfied with the blessings of thy house,
Thy holy temple!

5 By wonderful deeds dost thou answer us in mercy,
O God of our salvation!
Who art the confidence of all the ends of the earth,
And of the most distant seas!
6 Thou makest fast the mountains by thy power,
Being girded with might!
7 Thou stillest the roaring of the seas, the roaring of their
waves,
And the tumult of the peoples.
8 They also that dwell in the uttermost parts are awed by
thy signs;
Thou makest the outgoings of the morning and evening
to rejoice.

9 Thou visitest the earth, and waterest it,
Thou enrichest it exceedingly;
The river of God is full of water:
Thou providest them corn, when thou hast thus prepared
the earth.
10 Thou waterest its furrows abundantly;
Thou settlest its ridges:
Thou makest it soft with showers;
Thou blessest its increase.
11 Thou crownest the year with thy goodness;
And thy paths drop fatness.
12 They drop upon the pastures of the wilderness:
And the hills are girded with gladness.
13 The pastures are clothed with flocks;
The valleys are covered over with corn;
They shout for joy, they also sing.

23.   *PSALM LXVII.*

Prayer for God's blessing.

A Psalm. A Song.

1 God be merciful unto us, and bless us,
  And cause his face to shine upon us;   [Selah]
2 That thy way may be known upon earth,
  Thy salvation among all nations.
3 Let the peoples praise thee, O God!
  Let all the peoples praise thee!
4 O let the nations be glad and sing for joy:
  For thou dost judge the people with equity,
  And govern the nations upon earth.   [Selah]
5 Let the peoples praise thee, O God!
  Yea, let all the peoples praise thee!
6 The earth hath yielded her increase,
  God, our God, hath blessed us.
7 May God continue to bless us,
  And may all the ends of the earth fear him!

24.   *PSALM LXXIII.*

*A didactic poem on the perplexing problem of the apparent prosperity of the
wicked.   The psalmist himself once troubled with this problem
gives the result of his reflections thereon.*

A Psalm of Asaph.

1 Surely God is good to Israel,—
  To those who are pure in heart.
2 But as for me, my feet almost gave way;
  My steps had well nigh slipped.
3 For I was envious of the proud,
  When I saw the prosperity of the wicked.

4 For they have no pains even to their death;
  But their strength is firm. ·
5 They are not in the troubles of other men;

Neither are they plagued like other men.

6 Therefore pride is as a chain about their neck;
Violence covereth them as a garment.

7 Their eyes stand out with fatness;
They have more than heart could wish.

8 They scoff, and in wickedness utter oppression;
They speak haughtily.

9 They have set their mouth against the heavens,
And their tongue goeth through the earth.

10 Therefore his people turn hither:
And water in abundance is swallowed down by them.

11 And they say, "How doth God know?
And is there knowledge in the Most High?

12 Behold, these are the wicked;
Yet they are ever at ease, they increase in riches.

13 Surely in vain have I cleansed my heart,
And washed my hands in innocence.

14 For all the day long have I been plagued,
And my chastisement was every morning."

15 If I had said, I will speak like them,
Behold, I should be treacherous to the generation of thy
children.

16 Yet when I mused in order to understand this,
It was too difficult in mine eyes;

17 Until I went into the sanctuary of God,
And considered their latter end.

18 Surely thou settest them in slippery places;
Thou castest them down to destruction.

19 How are they become a desolation in a moment!
They are utterly consumed with terrors.

20 As a dream when one awaketh,
So, O LORD! when thou awakest, thou wilt make their vain
show a derision.

21 When my heart was grieved,
And I felt as if wounded in my reins:

22 Then was I stupid and without understanding ;
   I was like one of the brutes before thee.
23 Nevertheless I am continually with thee ;
   Thou hast holden my right hand.
24 Thou shalt guide me with thy counsel,
   And at last receive me to glory.
25 Whom have I in heaven but thee?
   And there is none upon earth that I desire beside thee.
26 Though my flesh and my heart fail :
   God is the strength of my heart and my portion for ever.
27 For, lo, they that are far from thee perish ;
   Thou destroyest all who estrange themselves from thee.
28 But it is good for me to draw near unto God ;
   I have made the LORD GOD my refuge,
   That I may tell of all thy works.

25. *PSALM LXXXI.*

A call to the worship of the true God on the great festivals. The psalmist hears the voice of God, reminding of the deliverance from Egypt, warning against idolatry, rebuking the people for their disobedience and promising them protection and blessing if they would persistently seek and honestly serve him.

A Psalm of Asaph.

1 Sing aloud unto God, our strength !
   Shout joyfully unto the God of Jacob !
2 Raise a song, and strike the timbrel,
   The pleasant harp, and the psaltery !
3 Blow the trumpet in the new moon,
   At the full moon, on our solemn feast day !
4 For it is a statute for Israel,
   An ordinance of the God of Jacob.
5 He appointed it in Joseph for a testimony,
   When he went out over the land of Egypt.—
   The language of one I know not do I hear :

6 " I removed his shoulder from the burden ;
His hands were freed from the basket.
7 Thou didst call in trouble, and I delivered thee ;
I answered thee in the secret place of thunder ;
I proved thee at the waters of Meribah.   [Selah]
8 Hear, O my people, and I will admonish thee !
O Israel, if thou wouldst hearken unto me !
9 There shall no strange god be in thee ;
Neither shalt thou worship any foreign god !
10 I am the LORD thy God,
Who brought thee out of the land of Egypt :
Open thy mouth wide, and I will fill it !
11 But my people would not hearken to my voice ;
And Israel was not willing to follow me.
12 So I let them go after the stubbornness of their heart,
That they might walk in their own counsels.

13 " Oh that my people would hearken unto me,
That Israel would walk in my ways !
14 I should soon subdue their enemies,
And turn my hand against their adversaries.
15 The haters of the LORD should submit themselves unto him ;
But their time should endure for ever.
16 I should feed them also with the finest of the wheat ;
And with honey out of the rock should I satisfy thee."

26.   *PSALM LXXXII.*

*This Psalm rebukes corrupt judges and reminds them that God holds them
responsible for the faithful administration of justice.*

A Psalm of Asaph.

1 God standeth in the congregation of God ;
He judgeth among the judges.
2 " How long will ye judge unjustly,
And respect the persons of the wicked?   [Selah.]

3 Judge the poor and fatherless ;
  Do justice to the afflicted and destitute.
4 Rescue the poor and needy ;
  Deliver them out of the hand of the wicked.
5 They know not, neither do they understand ;
  They walk in darkness :
  All the foundations of the land are shaken.
6 I said, Ye are gods,
  And all of you sons of the Most High.
7 Nevertheless ye shall die like men,
  And fall like one of the princes." · ·
8 Arise, O God, judge the earth !
  For thou hast dominion over all the nations.

27.   *PSALM LXXXIV.*

Love and longing for the worship of God in the sanctuary.

A Psalm of the Sons of Korah.

1 How lovely are thy tabernacles,
  O LORD of hosts !
2 My soul longeth, yea, fainteth for the courts of the LORD ;
  My heart and my flesh cry aloud for the living God.
3 Yea, the sparrow findeth an abode,
  And the swallow a nest for herself, where she may lay her
      young,
  Even thine altars, O LORD of hosts,
  My King, and my God !
4 Happy are they who dwell in thy house,
  Who are continually praising thee.   [Selah.]
5 Happy is the man whose strength is in thee ;
  In whose heart are the highways to Zion.
6 Passing through the valley of Weeping they make it a place
      of springs ;
  Yea, the early rain covereth it with blessings.
7 They go on from strength to strength,
  Every one of them appeareth before God in Zion.

8 O LORD, God of hosts, hear my prayer,
  Give ear, O God of Jacob!   [Selah]
9 Behold, O God, our shield,
  And look upon the face of thine anointed !
10 For a day in thy courts is better than a thousand ;
  I would rather stand at the threshold of the house of my
      God,
  Than dwell in the tents of wickedness.
11 For the LORD God is a sun and a shield ;
  The LORD will give grace and glory :
  No good thing will he withhold from them that walk up
      rightly.
12 O LORD of hosts,
  Happy is the man who trusteth in thee !

28.   *PSALM LXXXV.*

Prayer for the complete restoration of Israel after the return from the
captivity, and for God's renewed favor and blessing.

A Psalm of the Sons of Korah.

1 O LORD ! thou hast been favorable unto thy land ;
  Thou hast brought back the captivity of Jacob.
2 Thou hast forgiven the iniquity of thy people,
  Thou hast covered all their sin.   [Selah.]
3 Thou hast taken away all thy wrath,
  Thou hast turned thyself from the fierceness of thine anger.
4 Restore us, O God of our salvation,
  And cause thine indignation toward us to cease !
5 Wilt thou be angry with us for ever?
  Wilt thou draw out thine anger to all generations?
6 Wilt thou not quicken us again,
  That thy people may rejoice in thee?
7 Show us thy mercy, O LORD,
  And grant us thy salvation !

8 I will hear what God the Lord will speak:
  For he will speak peace to his people, and to his servants;
  But let them not turn again to folly!
9 Surely his salvation is nigh them that fear him;
  That glory may dwell in our land.
10 Mercy and truth shall meet together;
  Righteousness and peace shall kiss each other.
11 Truth shall spring out of the earth;
  And righteousness shall look down from heaven.
12 Yea, the Lord shall give that which is good;
  And our land shall yield her increase.
13 Righteousness shall go before him,
  And set us in the way of his steps.

29.   *PSALM LXXXVI.*

The distressed poet prays for divine help and guidance, and for a new token of God's grace and mercy.

A Prayer of David.

1 Incline thine ear, O Lord! and answer me,
  For I am poor and distressed.
2 Preserve my life, for I am devoted to thee;
  O thou, my God! save thy servant who trusteth in thee.
3 Be merciful unto me, O Lord!
  For unto thee do I cry all the day long.
4 Rejoice the soul of thy servant;
  For unto thee, O Lord! do I lift up my soul.
5 For thou, Lord, art good and ready to forgive,
  And rich in mercy unto all them that call upon thee.
6 Give ear, O Lord! unto my prayer;
  And hearken unto the voice of my supplications!
7 In the day of my trouble I will call upon thee;
  For thou wilt answer me.
8 There is none like unto thee among the gods, O Lord!
  Neither are there any works like unto thy works.

9 All nations whom thou hast made shall come and worship
    before thee, O LORD!
    And they shall glorify thy name.

10 For thou art great, and doest wondrous things;
    Thou art God alone.

11 Teach me thy way, O LORD!   I will walk in thy truth;
    Unite my heart to fear thy name.

12 I will praise thee, O LORD, my God! with my whole heart;
    And I will glorify thy name for evermore.

13 For great is thy mercy toward me;
    And thou hast delivered my soul from the lowest pit

14 O God! the proud are risen up against me,
    And the congregation of violent men have sought after my
      soul,
    And have not set thee before them.

15 But thou, O LORD! art a God full of compassion and gra-
    cious,
    Slow to anger and rich in mercy and truth.

16 O turn unto me, and have mercy upon me;
    Give thy strength unto thy servant,
    And save the son of thine handmaid.

17 Show me a token for good;
    That they who hate me may see it, and be ashamed,
    Because thou, O LORD, helpest and comfortest me!

30.   *PSALM XC.*

*The eternity of God contrasted to the frailty of man.   Prayer for divine
mercy and forbearance.*

A Prayer of Moses, the man of God.

1 LORD! thou hast been a place of refuge unto us
    In all generations!

2 Before the mountains were brought forth,
    Or ever thou hadst formed the earth and the world,
    Even from everlasting to everlasting thou art God!

3 But man thou turnest again to dust,
  And sayest, " Return, ye children of men ! "
4 For a thousand years in thy sight
  Are but as yesterday when it is past,
  And as a watch in the night.
5 Thou carriest them away as with a flood, they are as a sleep ;
  In the morning they are like grass which groweth up.
6 In the morning it flourisheth and shooteth up,
  In the evening it is cut down and withered.

7 For we are consumed in thine anger,
  And in thy wrath are we troubled.
8 Thou hast set our iniquities before thee,
  Our secret sins in the light of thy countenance.
9 For all our days are passed away in thy wrath ;
  We spend our years like a thought.
10 The days of our years are threescore years and ten,
  Or even, by reason of strength, fourscore years ;
  Yet is their pride but weariness and sorrow ;
  For it vanisheth swiftly, and we fly away.

11 Who knoweth the power of thine anger,
  And thy wrath according to the fear that is due unto thee?
12 So teach us to number our days,
  That we may get us a heart of wisdom.

13 Return, O Lord ! how long—?
  And have compassion upon thy servants !
14 O satisfy us in the morning with thy mercy ;
  That we may rejoice and be glad all our days.
15 Make us glad according to the days wherein thou hast
    afflicted us,
  And the years wherein we have seen adversity.
16 Let thy work appear unto thy servants,
  And thy glory upon their children.
17 And let the favor of the Lord, our God, be upon us,
  And establish thou the work of our hands upon us ;
  Yea, the work of our hands establish thou it !

31.   *PSALM XCI.*

*The safety of him who puts his trust in God.**

1 He who sitteth in the shelter of the Most High
  Abideth in the shadow of the Almighty.
2 "I say to the Lord, Thou art my refuge and my fortress;
  My God, in whom I trust!"
3 Surely he shall deliver thee from the snare of the fowler.
  And from the wasting pestilence.
4 He shall cover thee with his pinions,
  And under his wings shalt thou take refuge;
  His truth is a shield and a buckler.
5 Thou shalt not be afraid of the terror by night,
  Nor of the arrow that flieth by day.
6 Of the pestilence that walketh in darkness,
  Nor of the destruction that wasteth at noonday.
7 A thousand shall fall at thy side,
  And ten thousand at thy right hand;
  But it shall not come nigh thee.
8 Only with thine eyes shalt thou behold,
  And see the reward of the wicked.

9 "Yea, thou, O Lord, art my refuge!"
  Thou hast made the Most High thy protection.
10 There shall no evil befall thee,
  Neither shall any plague come nigh thy tent.
11 For he shall give his angels charge over thee,
  To keep thee in all thy ways.
12 They shall bear thee up in their hands,
  Lest thou dash thy foot against a stone.
13 Thou shalt tread upon the lion and adder;
  The young lion and the serpent thou shalt trample under
    foot.

---

*This psalm is supposed to have been a Temple song performed by a chorus and single voices in the following way:
  Chorus. v. 1; single voice, v. 2; chorus, vs. 3-8; single voice, the first part of **v.9**; chorus from the second part of v. 9 to v. 13; single voice speaking in the name of God vs. 14-10.

14 "Because he loveth me, I will deliver him;
I will set him on high, because he knoweth my name.
15 He shall call upon me, and I will answer him"
I will be with him in trouble;
I will deliver him, and bring him to honor.
16 With long life will I satisfy him,
And show him my salvation."

32. *PSALM XCII.*

*Praise is due to God under whose just government the wicked is flourishing
but for a day, soon to perish; while the righteous is flourishing
and blessed even in old age.*

A Psalm, a Song for the Sabbath day.

1 It is a good thing to give thanks unto the LORD,
And to sing praises unto thy name, O Most High!
2 To show forth thy loving kindness in the morning,
And thy faithfulness every night.
3 Upon the ten-stringed instrument and the lute,
Upon the harp with a solemn sound.
4 For thou, LORD, hast made me glad by thy doings;
In the works of thy hands I greatly rejoice!

5 How great are thy works, O LORD!
Thy thoughts are very deep.
6 A brutish man knoweth it not,
Neither doth a fool understand this.
7 When the wicked spring up like grass,
And all the workers of iniquity do flourish,
It is but to be destroyed forever.
8 But thou, O LORD, art forever exalted!
9 For, lo, thine enemies, O LORD!
For, lo, thine enemies perish;
All the workers of iniquity are scattered!
10 But my horn thou exaltest like the buffalo's;
I am anointed with fresh oil.

11 Mine eye looketh [calmly] on mine enemies,
   Mine ears do [fearlessly] hear when the wicked rise against
   me.

12 The righteous shall flourish like the palm tree;
   He shall grow up like a cedar in Lebanon.
13 They that are planted in the house of the LORD
   Shall flourish in the courts of our God.
14 They shall still bring forth fruit in old age;
   They shall be full of sap and green:
15 To show that the LORD is upright;
   He is my rock, and there is no unrighteousness in him.

33.   *PSALM XCIII.*

The majesty and glory of God whose eternal power governs the universe.

1 The LORD reigneth; he is clothed with majesty;
   The LORD is clothed with majesty, girded with strength:
   The world also is established that it can not be moved.
2 Thy throne is established of old;
   Thou art from everlasting!

3 The floods, lift up, O LORD!
   The floods lift up their voice;
   The floods lift up their roaring!
4 Above the voices of many waters,
   The mighty breakers of the sea,
   The LORD on high is mighty.

5 Thy testimonies are very sure;
   Holiness becometh thine house,
   O LORD, for ever more!

34.   *PSALM XCV.*

Exhortation to praise God and to obey him.

1 O come, let us sing unto the LORD;
   Let us shout joyfully to the rock of our salvation!

2 Let us come before his presence with thanksgiving,
And sing joyfully to him with psalms !

3 For the LORD is a great God,
And a great King above all gods.
4 In his hand are the deep places of the earth;
The heights of the mountains are his also.
5 The sea is his, and he made it ;
And his hands formed the dry land.

6 O come, let us worship and bow down !
Let us kneel before the LORD our maker !
7 For he is our God,
And we are the people of his pasture, and the flock of his
hand.
O that ye would now hear his voice !

8 "Harden not your heart, as at Meribah, *
As in the day of Massah in the wilderness :
9 Where your fathers tempted me,
And tried me, although they had seen my work.
10 Forty years long was I grieved with that generation,
And I said, 'They are a people of a perverse heart,
And they know not my ways.'
11 Therefore I swore in my wrath,
That they should not enter into my rest."

35. *PSALM XCVI.*

*General summons to sing the praises of Him who is the true and only God.
All the nations are exhorted to worship Him, and the whole creation is called upon to rejoice before Him who governs
and judges the world in justice.*

1 O sing unto the LORD a new song;
Sing unto the LORD, all the earth !

*In this and the following verses the Supreme Being is introduced as warning
Israel not to follow the example of their forefathers in the wilderness.—Meribah,
meaning strife, and Massah meaning temptation, were the significant names given
to a place in the wilderness where Israel tempted God. See Exodus xvii. 1-7.

2 Sing unto the Lord, praise his name ;
Show forth his salvation from day to day

3 Proclaim his glory among the nations,
His marvelous works among all the peoples !

4 For great is the Lord, and highly to be praised,
He is to be feared above all gods.

5 For all the gods of the peoples are idols ;
But the Lord made the heavens.

6 Glory and majesty are before him ;
Strength and beauty are in his sanctuary.

7 Give unto the Lord, ye tribes of the people,
Give unto the Lord honor and praise !

8 Give unto the Lord the honor due unto his name ;
Bring an offering, and come into his courts !

9 O worship the Lord in the beauty of holiness !
Tremble before him, all the earth !

10 Say among the nations, The Lord reigneth ;
The world also is established that it can not be moved ;
He shall judge the peoples with equity.

11 Let the heavens be glad, and let the earth rejoice ;
Let the sea roar, and the fullness thereof ;

12 Let the field exult, and all that is therein ;
Then shall all the trees of the wood sing for joy ;

13 Before the Lord, for he cometh ;
For he cometh to judge the earth :
He shall judge the world with righteousness,
And the peoples in his truth.

36. *PSALM XCVII.*

*The majesty of God who judges the world. At His judgments the idolators
are terrified, while his true worshipers rejoice. Exhortation to
righteousness which alone gains the divine grace.*

1 The Lord reigneth ; let the earth rejoice !
Let the multitude of isles be glad !

2 Clouds ana darkness are round about him;
  Righteousness and judgment are the foundation of his
    throne.
3 A fire goeth before him,
  And burneth up his adversaries round about.
4 His lightnings illumine the world;
  The earth beholdeth and trembleth.
5 The mountains melt like wax at the presence of the LORD,
  At the presence of the LORD of the whole earth.
6 The heavens declare his righteousness,
  And all the nations behold his glory.

7 Ashamed are all who serve graven images,
  Who glory in idols:
  Unto him bow down all the gods.
8 Zion heard it and is glad,
  And the daughters of Judah rejoice,
  Because of thy judgments, O LORD!
9 For thou, LORD, art most high above all the earth;
  Thou art exalted far above all gods!

10 O ye that love the LORD, hate evil!
  He preserveth the souls of his pious servants;
  He delivereth them from the hand of the wicked.
11 Light is sown for the righteous,
  And gladness for the upright in heart.
12 Be glad in the LORD, ye righteous;
  And give thanks to his holy name!

37. *PSALM C.*

*A temple song calling on all to serve God cheerfully and to give thanks for
His everlasting mercy.*

A Psalm of Thanksgiving.

1 Shout joyfully unto the LORD, all ye lands!
2 Serve the LORD with gladness;
  Come before his presence with singing!

3 Know ye that the LORD is God!
  It is he that hath made us, and we are his;
  We are his people, and the flock of his pasture.
4 Enter into his gates with thanksgiving,
  And into his courts with praise;
  Give thanks unto him, and bless his name!
5 For the LORD is good, his mercy endureth forever;
  And his faithfulness unto all generations.

38.   *PSALM CI.*

*David expresses his noble purposes as to his religious life and regal respon-
sibilities.*

A Psalm of David.

1 I will sing of mercy and justice;
  Unto thee, O LORD! will I sing praises.
2 I will carefully regard the way of uprightness:—
  Oh, when wilt thou come unto me?—
  I will walk within my house with an upright heart.
3 I will set no base thing before mine eyes:
  I hate the work of them that turn aside;
  It shall not cleave unto me.
4 A froward heart shall depart from me;
  I will know no evil thing.
5 Whoso privily slandereth his neighbor, him will I destroy;
  Him that hath a haughty look and a proud heart will I not
      suffer.
6 Mine eyes shall be upon the faithful of the land, that they
      may dwell with me;
  He that walketh in the way of uprightness, he shall serve me.
7 He that worketh deceit shall not dwell within my house;
  He that speaketh falsehood shall not remain in my sight.
8 Morning by morning will I destroy all the wicked of the land;
  To cut off all the workers of iniquity from the city of the
      LORD.

39. *PSALM CIII.*

Grateful homage to God for His redeeming and forgiving mercies toward individuals as well as his people. After contrasting human frailty with this everlasting mercy of the eternal ruler of the universe, all heavenly and earthly beings are called upon to join in his praise.

A Psalm of David

1 Bless the LORD, O my soul !
  And all that is within me, bless his holy name !
2 Bless the LORD, O my soul !
  And forget not all his benefits !
3 Who forgiveth all thine iniquities ;
  Who healeth all thy diseases :
4 Who redeemeth thy life from destruction ;
  Who crowneth thee with loving kindness and tender mercies :
5 Who satisfieth thine old age with good,
  So that thy youth is renewed like the eagle's.

6 The LORD executeth righteous acts,
  And judgments for all that are oppressed.
7 He made known his ways unto Moses,
  His doings unto the children of Israel.
8 The LORD is full of compassion and gracious,
  Slow to anger, and plenteous in mercy.
9 He will not always chide ;
  Neither will he keep his anger for ever.
10 He hath not dealt with us after our sins,
  Nor rewarded us after our iniquities.

11 For as the heaven is high above the earth,
  So great is his mercy toward them that fear him.
12 As far as the east is from the west,
  So far hath he removed our transgressions from us.
13 Even as a father pitieth his children,
  So the LORD pitieth them that fear him.
14 For he knoweth our frame ;
  He remembereth that we are dust.

15 As for man, his days are as grass;
   As a flower of the field, so he flourisheth.
16 For the wind passeth over it, and it is gone;
   And the place thereof shall know it no more.
17 But the mercy of the LORD is from everlasting to everlasting upon them that fear him,
   And his righteousness unto children's children;
18 To such as keep his covenant,
   And to those that remember his precepts to do them.

19 The LORD hath established his throne in the heavens;
   And his kingdom ruleth over all.
20 Bless the LORD, ye angels of his:
   Ye mighty in strength, who fulfill his word,
   Hearkening unto the voice of his word!
21 Bless the LORD, all ye his hosts;
   Ye ministers of his, who do his pleasure!
22 Bless the LORD, all ye his works,
   In all places of his dominion!
   Bless the LORD, O my soul!

40.   *PSALM CIV.*

Praise to God, the glorious Creator of the world. *

1 Bless the LORD, O my soul!
  O LORD, my God, thou art very great!
  Thou art clothed with glory and majesty!

---

*The following synopsis will assist the reader in comprehending the sublime contents of this grand psalm, which is one of the brightest gems in the crown of Biblical poetry:

After a short prelude in praise of God's glory and majesty (v. 1) the psalmist de- scribes poetically the creation of light, heaven and earth (vs. 2-5.), the separation of land and water (vs. 6-9) and God's providing care for man and beast (vs. 10-18). Then he mentions the sun and the moon and the changes of day and night with their changing scenes (vs. 19-23); furthermore how God filled even the sea with living creatures (vs. 24-26) and how the life of all beings depends upon Him (vs. 27-30). Impressed with the glory of God whose power is also manifested in earth- quakes and volcanoes, the psalmist avows his purpose to sing His praise continually, and closes with the wish that all sin may cease from the earth, so that every soul may join him in praising the eternal God (vs. 31-35).

2 He covereth himself with light as with a garment;
  He spreadeth out the heavens like a curtain ;
3 He layeth the beams of his chambers in the waters;
  He maketh the clouds his chariot;
  He rideth upon the wings of the wind.
4 He maketh the winds his messengers ;
  The flaming lightnings his ministers.
5 He established the earth on its foundations ;
  It shall not be moved forever.

6 Thou didst cover it with the deep as with a garment;
  The waters stood above the mountains.
7 At thy rebuke they fled ;
  At the voice of thy thunder they hasted away ;
8 The mountains rose, the valleys sank ;
  In the place which thou didst appoint for them.
9 Thou hast set a bound that they may not pass over;
  That they turn not again to cover the earth.

10 He sendeth forth springs into the valleys ;
   They run among the mountains:
11 They give drink to every beast of the field ;
   The wild asses quench their thirst.
12 By them the fowl of the heaven have their habitation,
   They sing among the branches.
13 He watereth the mountains from his chambers :
   The earth is satisfied with the fruit of thy works !

14 He causeth the grass to grow for the cattle,
   And herb for the service of man ;
   That he may bring forth food out of the earth :
15 And wine that maketh glad the heart of man,
   And oil to make his face to shine,
   And bread that strengtheneth man's heart.
16 The trees of the LORD are full of sap,
   The cedars of Lebanon, which he hath planted ;
17 There the birds make their nests :
   As for the stork, the cypresses are her house.

18 The high mountains are for the wild goats;
   The rocks are a refuge for the conies.

19 He appointeth the moon for seasons:
   The sun knoweth his going down.
20 Thou makest darkness, and it is night;
   Wherein all the beasts of the forest do creep forth.
21 The young lions roar after their prey,
   And seek their food from God.
22 The sun ariseth, they withdraw themselves,
   And lie down in their dens.
23 Man goeth forth unto his work,
   And to his labor until the evening.

24 O Lord, how manifold are thy works!
   In wisdom hast thou made them all,
   The earth is full of thy riches!
25 Yonder is the sea, great and wide,
   Therein are moving creatures without number,
   Both small and great beasts.
26 There go the ships;
   There is leviathan, which thou hast made to play therein.

27 These wait all upon thee,
   That thou mayest give them their food in due season.
28 Thou givest it unto them, they gather it;
   Thou openest thine hand, they are satisfied with good.
29 Thou hidest thy face, they are troubled;
   Thou takest away their breath, they die,
   And return to their dust.
30 Thou sendeth forth thy spirit, they are created;
   And thou renewest the face of the earth.

31 The glory of the Lord shall endure forever;
   The Lord shall rejoice in his works!
32 He looketh on the earth, and it trembleth;
   He toucheth the mountains, and they smoke.

33 I will sing unto the LORD as long as I live;
   I will sing praise to my God while I have my being.
34 May my meditation be agreeable to him !
   I will rejoice in the LORD.
35 May sinners cease from the earth,
   And the wicked be no more !
   Bless the LORD, O my soul !
   Hallelujah !

41.   *PART OF PSALM CVII.*

(vs. 21-32.)

*Admonishing to render thanks for divine protection under the perils of a sea
storm.*

1 O that men would praise the LORD for his goodness,
  For his wonderful works to the children of men !
2 Let them offer the sacrifices of thanksgiving,
  And declare his work with singing !

3 They who go down to the sea in ships,
  And do business in great waters,
4 These see the works of the LORD,
  And his wonders in the deep.
5 For he commandeth, and raiseth the stormy wind,
  Which lifteth up the waves thereof.
6 They mount up to the heaven, they go down again to the
       depths;
  Their soul melteth with distress.
7 They reel to and fro, and stagger like a drunken man,
  And all their skill is exhausted.
8 Then they cry unto the LORD in their trouble,
  And he bringeth them out of their distresses.
9 He maketh the storm a calm,
  So that the waves thereof are still.
10 Then are they glad because they be quiet;
   So he bringeth them to their desired haven.

11 O let them praise the Lord for his goodness,
For his wonderful works to the children of men !
12 Let them exalt him in the congregation of the people,
And praise him in the assembly of the elders !

42. *PSALM CXI.*

Praising God for his gracious works, especially in guiding Israel.*

1 Hallelujah !
I will give thanks unto the Lord with my whole heart,
In the assembly of the upright, and in the congregation.
2 The works of the Lord are great,
Sought out of all them that have pleasure therein.
3 His work is glorious and majestic,
And his righteousness endureth forever.
4 He hath made his wonderful works to be remembered ;
The Lord is gracious and full of compassion.
5 He hath given meat unto them that fear him ;
He will ever be mindful of his covenant.
6 He showed his people the power of his works,
In giving them the heritage of the nations.
7 The works of his hands are truth and justice ;
All his precepts are sure.
8 They stand firm for ever and ever ;
They are founded in truth and uprightness.
9 He hath sent redemption unto his people ;
He hath established his covenant forever ;
Holy and to be feared is his name.
10 The fear of the Lord is the beginning of wisdom ;
A good understanding have all they that keep his com-
mandments ;
His praise endureth forever.

---

* This and the succeeding psalm are, in the original, alphabetically arranged,
each clause in them beginning with a different letter, according to the order of the
Hebrew alphabet. In consequence of this artificial arrangement, the sentences are,
at times, only loosely connected.

43. *PSALM CXII.*

The happiness of the righteous and charitable man.

1 Hallelujah !
Happy is the man who feareth the LORD,
Who delighteth greatly in his commandments.
2 His posterity shall be mighty on the earth ;
The generation of the upright shall be blessed.
3 Wealth and riches are in his house,
And his righteousness endureth forever.
4 Unto the upright there ariseth light in the darkness ;
He is gracious, and full of compassion, and righteous.
5 Well is it with the man that dealeth graciously and lendeth ;
He shall maintain his cause in judgment.
6 For he shall never be moved ;
The righteous shall be in everlasting remembrance.
7 He shall not be afraid of evil tidings ;
His heart is firm, trusting in the LORD.
8 His heart is established, he shall not be afraid,
Even when he looketh on his assailants.
9 He hath scattered blessings, he hath given to the needy ;
His righteousness endureth forever.
His horn shall be exalted with honor.
10 The wicked seeth it, and is grieved ;
He gnasheth his teeth, and melteth away ;
The desire of the wicked perisheth.

44. *PSALM CXIII.**

An exhortation to praise God for His condescending goodness.

1 Hallelujah !
Praise, O ye servants of the LORD !
Praise the name of the LORD !

*This and the five succeeding psalms constitute the so-called *Hallel*, which may have been designed for the celebration of the feast of Passover, but is still now recited at the divine service on the three festivals, as well as on Rosh Chodesh and Chanuka.

2 Blessed be the name of the LORD
From this time forth and for evermore ɪ
3 From the rising of the sun unto its going down
May the LORD's name be praised !

4 The LORD is high above all nations,
And his glory above the heavens.
5 Who is like unto the LORD, our God,
That hath his seat on high,
6 That looketh down low
Upon the heavens and the earth ?
7 He raiseth the poor from the dust,
And lifeth up the needy from the dunghill ;
8 That he may set him with princes,
Even with the princes of his people.
9 He causeth the barren woman to dwell in a house,
A joyful mother of children.
Hallelujah !

45. *PSALM CXIV.*

A glorious song on Israel's departure from Egypt, under the guidance of God.

1 When Israel went forth from Egypt,
The house of Jacob from a people of strange language ;
2 Judah became his sanctuary,
Israel his dominion.
3 The sea saw it, and fled ;
The Jordan was driven back.
4 The mountains skipped like rams,
The little hills like lambs.

5 What aileth thee, O thou sea, that thou fleest?
Thou, Jordan, that thou turnest back ?
6 Ye mountains, that ye skip like rams ;
Ye little hills, like lambs ?

7 Tremble, thou earth, at the presence of the LORD,
  At the presence of the God of Jacob;
8 Who turned the rock into a pool of water,
  The flint into a fountain of waters!

46.　　　　　　*PSALM CXV.*

Prayer that God would display his glory as the true God, by giving aid to
his people against the worshipers of idols.

1 Not unto us, O LORD! not unto us,
  But unto thy name give glory,
  For thy mercy, and for thy truth's sake!
2 Wherefore should the nations say,
  "Where is now their God?"
3 But our God is in the heavens;
  He doeth whatsoever he pleaseth.

4 Their idols are silver and gold,
  The work of men's hands.
5 They have mouths, but they speak not;
  Eyes have they, but they see not:
6 They have ears, but they hear not;
  Noses have they, but they smell not;
7 They have hands, but they handle not;
  Feet have they, but they walk not;
  Neither speak they through their throat.
8 They that make them shall be like unto them;
  Yea, every one that trusteth in them.

9 O Israel! trust thou in the LORD!
  He is their help and their shield.
10 O house of Aaron! trust ye in the LORD!
  He is their help and their shield.
11 Ye that fear the LORD, trust in the LORD!
  He is their help and their shield.

12 The LORD hath been mindful of us; he will bless us;
He will bless the house of Israel;
He will bless the house of Aaron.
13 He will bless them that fear the LORD,
Both small and great.
14 The LORD increase you more and more,
You and your children.
15 Blessed are ye of the LORD,
Who made heaven and earth.

16 The heavens are the heavens of the LORD;
But the earth hath he given to the children of men.
17 The dead praise not the LORD,
Neither any that go down into silence;
18 But we will bless the LORD
From this time forth and for evermore!
Hallelujah!

47.   *PSALM CXVI.*

Thanksgiving song for deliverance from calamity.

1 I love the LORD because he hath heard
My voice and my supplications.
2 Because he hath inclined his ear unto me,
Therefore will I call upon him as long as I live.
3 The snares of death compassed me,
And the pains of the under world seized upon me;
I found trouble and sorrow.
4 Then called I upon the name of the LORD:
" O LORD! I beseech thee; deliver my soul!"
5 Gracious is the LORD, and righteous;
Yea our God is merciful.
6 The LORD preserveth the simple;
I was brought low, and he saved me.

7 Return unto thy rest, O my soul!
For the LORD hath dealt bountifully with thee.

8 For thou hast delivered my soul from death,
Mine eyes from tears,
And my feet from falling.
9* I will walk before the LORD
In the land of the living.
10 I had trust, although I said,
" I am greatly afflicted !"
11 I said in my distress,
" All men are false."

12 What shall I render unto the LORD
For all his benefits toward me?
13 I will take the cup of salvation,
And call upon the name of the LORD.
14 I will pay my vows unto the LORD,
Yea, in the presence of all his people.
15 Precious in the sight of the LORD
Is the death of his pious ones.
16 O LORD ! truly I am thy servant ;
I am thy servant, the son of thy handmaid :
Thou hast loosed my bonds.
17 I will offer to thee the sacrifice of thanksgiving,
And will call upon the name of the LORD.
18 I will pay my vows unto the LORD,
Yea, in the presence of all his people ;
19 In the courts of the LORD's house,
In the midst of thee, O Jerusalem !
Hallelujah !

48. *PSALM CXVII.*

Exhorting all nations to praise God.

1 O praise the LORD, all ye nations !
Laud him, all ye peoples !
2 For his mercy is great toward us ;
And the truth of the LORD endureth for ever.
Hallelujah !

49.   *PSALM CXVIII.*

*Public thanksgiving for deliverance from danger and victory over enemies.**

1 O give thanks unto the LORD, for he is good ;
Yea, his mercy endureth for ever !
2 Let Israel now say,
Yea, his mercy endureth for ever !
3 Let the house of Aaron now say,
Yea, his mercy endureth for ever !
4 Let them now that fear the LORD say,
Yea, his mercy endureth for ever !

5 Out of my distress I called upon the LORD:
The LORD answered me in delivering me.
6 The LORD is on my side, I will not fear ;
What can man do unto me?
7 The LORD is with me, as my helper ;
Therefore shall I [fearlessly] look on those who hate me.
8 It is better to trust in the LORD
Than to put confidence in man.
9 It is better to trust in the LORD
Than to put confidence in princes.

10 All nations compassed me about ;
In the name of the LORD I will cut them off.
11 They compassed me about ; yea, they compassed me about ;
In the name of the LORD I will cut them off

*This glorious song appears from its contents to have been composed on the occacasion of the entry of a festive procession into the temple courts to celebrate there some great victory. The song was probably performed by various choruses and single voices, in the following way:

Chorus calling upon all Israel to praise God (vs. 1-4). Single voice, speaking in the name of the people, expresses grateful acknowledgment for God's mercy, and confidence in him (vs. 5-9), describing the distress and the deliverance just experienced (vs. 10-18). Arrived at the gates of the inner court, permission to enter is asked (v. 19)and given (v. 20). Entering the gates, thanksgiving and prayer are offered (vs. 21-25). The High Priest (or a chorus of priests) receives the procession with a blessing, and orders the performance of sacrificial acts (vs. 26 27). Closing song of praise and thanksgiving (vs. 28-29.)

12 They compassed me about like bees; they are quenched as
the fire of thorns:
In the name of the LORD I will cut them off.
13 Thou didst thrust violently at me that I might fall;
But the LORD helped me.
14 The LORD is my strength and song;
And he is become my salvation.

15 The voice of rejoicing and salvation is in the tents of the
righteous:
" The right hand of the LORD doeth valiantly.
16 The right hand of the LORD is exalted;
The right hand of the LORD doeth valiantly."
17 I shall not die, but live,
And declare the works of the LORD.
18 The LORD hath sorely chastened me;
But he hath not given me over unto death.

19 Open to me the gates of righteousness;
I will enter into them, I will give thanks unto the LORD!
20 This is the gate of the LORD;
The righteous shall enter into it!

21 I will give thanks unto thee, for thou hast answered me,
And art become my salvation.
22 The stone which the builders rejected
Is become the chief corner-stone.
23 This is the LORD's doing;
It is marvellous in our eyes.
24 This is the day which the LORD hath made;
We will rejoice and be glad in it!
25 Save now, we beseech thee, O LORD!
O LORD, we beseech thee, send now prosperity!

26 " Blessed be he that cometh in the name of the LORD!
We bless you out of the house of the LORD."
27 The LORD is God, and he hath given us light:
Bind the sacrifice with cords, even unto the horns of the altar!

28 Thou art my God, and I will give thanks unto thee !
Thou art my God, I will exalt thee !
29 O give thanks unto the LORD, for he is good ;
Yea, his mercy endureth for ever !

50. *PSALM CXXI.*

Confidence in the protection of God.
A Pilgrim Song. *

1 I lift up mine eyes unto the mountains :
Whence shall my help come?
2 My help cometh from the LORD,
Who made heaven and earth.

3 He will not suffer thy foot to stumble ;
Thy guardian will not slumber.
4 Behold, the guardian of Israel
Doth neither slumber nor sleep.
5 The LORD is thy keeper ;
The LORD is thy shade at thy right hand.
6 The sun shall not smite thee by day,
Nor the moon by night.
7 The LORD shall keep thee from all evil ;
He shall keep thy soul.
8 The LORD shall keep thy going out and thy coming in,
From this time forth and for evermore.

51. *PSALM CXXII.*

Aspirations of love for the temple and for the scenes of worship there.
A Pilgrim Song, by David.

1 I was glad when they said unto me,
Let us go unto the house of the LORD !

*This is the second in a series of fifteen Psalms (120-134) each of which has the Hebrew heading, *Shir Hammaaloth.* The literal translation of this heading is " *Song of the Upgoings,*" or as the revised version renders it: Song of Ascents. The common version is: Song of Degrees. Some translate it with Song of the Pilgrimages or *Pilgrim Song.* These psalms are supposed to have been prepared to be sung when the people went up to Jerusalem to attend the three great annual festivals,

2 Our feet are standing
  Within thy gates, O Jerusalem !
3 Jerusalem, thou art [beautifully] built
  As a city that is compact together !
4 Thither the tribes go up, the tribes of the LORD,
  According to an ordinance for Israel,
  To give thanks unto the name of the LORD.
5 For there stand thrones for judgment,   .
  The thrones of the house of David.

6 Pray for the peace of Jerusalem !
  May they prosper who love thee !
7 Peace be within thy walls,
  And prosperity within thy palaces !
8 For the sake of my brethren and companions   ·
  I will now say, Peace be within thee !
9 For the sake of the house of the LORD our God
  I will seek thy good !

52.   *PSALM CXXIV.*

Praising God for having delivered Israel from a great calamity; probably
referring to the deliverance from the exile.

A Pilgrim Song by David.

1 If it had not been the LORD who was on our side,
  Let Israel now say,
2 If it had not been the LORD who was on our side,
  When men rose up against us :
3 Then they had swallowed us up alive,
  When their wrath was kindled against us :
4 Then the waters had overwhelmed us,
  The stream had gone over our soul ;
5 Then the proud waters had gone over our soul.

6 Blessed be the LORD,
  Who hath not given us as a prey to their teeth !

7 Our soul is escaped like a bird out of the snare of the fowlers ;
  The snare is broken, and we are escaped.
8 Our help is in the name of the LORD,
  Who made heaven and earth.

53.   *PSALM CXXVI.*

*Thanksgiving for the return from the captivity, and prayer for the complete
restoration of the exiles remaining at Babylon.*

A Pilgrim Song.

1 When the LORD brought back the captivity of Zion,
  We were like them that dream.
2 Then was our mouth filled with laughter,
  And our tongue with singing :
  Then said they among the nations,
  " The LORD hath done great things for them ! "
3 The LORD hath done great things for us ;
  Of which we are glad.

4 Bring back, O LORD ! our captivity,
  Like streams in the South !
5 They who sow in tears shall reap in joy.
6 Though he goeth forth weeping, bearing the seed ;
  He shall surely come back rejoicing, bringing his sheaves.

54.   *PSALM CXXVII.*

No happiness and prosperity without the blessing of God.

A Pilgrim Song by Solomon.

1 Except the LORD build the house,
  They labor in vain who build it :
  Except the LORD keep the city,
  The watchmen waketh but in vain.
2 It is vain for you that you rise up early, and go to rest late,
  And eat the bread of toil ;
  The same doth he give unto his beloved during sleep.

3 Behold, children are an heritage of the LORD,
  And offspring are his gift.
4 As arrows in the hand of a mighty man,
  So are the children of youth.
5 Happy is the man that hath his quiver full of them!
  They shall not be ashamed,
  When they speak with enemies in the gate.

55. *PSALM CXXVIII.*

The prosperity and domestic happiness of the religious man.

A Pilgrim Song.

1 Happy is every one who feareth the LORD,
  Who walketh in his ways!
2 Thou shalt eat the labor of thine hands;
  Happy shalt thou be, and it shall be well with thee!
.3 Thy wife shall be as a fruitful vine, within thy house;
  Thy children like olive plants, round about thy table.
4 Behold, that thus shall the man be blessed
  That feareth the LORD.
5 The LORD shall bless thee out of Zion,
  And thou shalt see the good of Jerusalem all the days of
      thy life.
6 Yea, thou shalt see thy children's children.
  Peace be upon Israel!

56. *PART OF PSALM CXXIX.*

God's help so often experienced by Israel in times of oppression.

A Pilgrim Song.

1 Much have they afflicted me from my youth up,
  May Israel now say;
2 Much have they afflicted me from my youth up,
  Yet they have not prevailed against me.
3 The plowers plowed upon my back;
  They made long their furrows.

4 But the LORD is righteous;
  He hath cut asunder the cords of the wicked.
5 They must be ashamed and turn back,
  All who hate Zion.

57.   *PSALM CXXX.*

Prayer for forgiveness, and expression of confidence in God.

A Pilgrim Song.

1 Out of the depths do I call unto thee, O LORD!
2 O Lord! listen to my voice.
  Let thine ears be attentive
  To the voice of my supplications!
3 If thou, LORD, shouldst mark iniquities,
  O Lord! who could stand?
4 But there is forgiveness with thee,
  That thou mayst be feared.

5 I hope for the LORD, my soul doth hope,
  And for his word do I wait.
6 My soul waiteth for the Lord,
  More than they who watch for the morning;
  Yea, more than they who watch for the morning!

7 O Israel, wait for the LORD!
  For with the LORD is mercy,
  And with him is plenteous redemption.
8 He will redeem Israel
  From all his iniquities.

58.   *PSALM CXXXI.*

Childlike resignation to God.

A Pilgrim Song by David.

1 O LORD! my heart is not haughty, nor mine eyes lofty;
  Neither do I exercise myself in great matters,
  Or in things too wonderful for me!

2 Verily I have stilled and quieted my soul;
Like a weaned child with his mother.
My soul is with me like a weaned child.

3 O Israel! wait for the LORD
From this time forth and forever more!

59. *PSALM CXXXIII.*

Praise of brotherly love and harmony.

A Pilgrim's Song, by David.

1 Behold, how good and how pleasant it is
For brethren to dwell together in unity!
2 It is like the precious oil upon the head,
That ran down upon the beard,
Even Aaron's beard,
That came down to the border of his garments;
3 Like the dew of Hermon,
Like that which cometh down upon the mountains of Zion:
For there the LORD commanded the blessing,
Even life for evermore.

60. *PART OF PSALM CXXXVII.*

Sad recollections of the time of the Babylonian Captivity.

1 By the rivers of Babylon,
There we sat down, yea, we wept,
When we remembered Zion.
2 Upon the willows in the midst thereof
We hanged up our harps.
3 For there they who led us captive required of us songs,
They who wasted us [required of us] mirth:
"Sing us one of the songs of Zion!"
4 How shall we sing the LORD's song
In a strange land?

5 If I forget thee, O Jerusalem,
  Let my right hand forget [her cunning]!
6 Let my tongue cleave to the roof of my mouth,
  If I remember thee not;
  If I prefer not Jerusalem
  Above my chief joy!

61. *PART OF PSALM CXXXIX.*

Vs. 1-12, 23-24.

God's Omniscience and Omnipresence.

A Psalm of David.

1 O LORD! thou searchest me, and knowest me!
2 Thou knowest my sitting down and my rising up,
  Thou understandest my thought afar off.
3 Thou seest my path and my lying-down,
  And art acquainted with all my ways.
4 For before the word is upon my tongue,
  Behold, O LORD! thou knowest it altogether!
5 Thou besettest me behind and before,
  And layest thy hand upon me.
6 Such knowledge is too wonderful for me;
  It is high, I can not attain unto it!

7 Whither shall I go from thy spirit?
  Or whither shall I flee from thy presence?
8 If I ascend up into heaven, thou art there!
  If I make my bed in the underworld, behold thou art there!
9 If I take the wings of the morning,
  And dwell in the uttermost parts of the sea;
10 Even there shall thy hand lead me,
  And thy right hand shall hold me!
11 If I say, "Surely the darkness shall cover me,"
  Even the night shall be light about me.
12 Yea, the darkness hideth not from thee,

But the night shineth as the day ;
The darkness and the light are both alike to thee.

* * * * * * *

13 Search me, O God, and know my heart ;
Try me, and know my thoughts :
14 And see if the way of trouble be within me,
And lead me in the way everlasting !

62. *PSALM CXLV.*

*Hymn in praise of the Almighty God for His righteous and merciful government and His all-bountiful providence.**

A Psalm of Praise, by David.

1 I will extol thee, my God, O King !
I will bless thy name for ever and ever !
2 Every day will I bless thee ;
And praise thy name for ever and ever !
3 Great is the Lord, and highly to be praised ;
Yea, his greatness is unsearchable.
4 One generation shall laud thy works to another,
And shall declare thy mighty deeds.

5 I will speak of the glorious honor of thy majesty,
And of thy wondrous works.
6 Men shall speak of the might of thy terrible deeds,
And I will declare thy greatness.
7 They shall pour forth the praise of thy great goodness,
And sing of thy righteousness.

8 The Lord is gracious, and full of compassion ;
Slow to anger, and great in mercy.
9 The Lord is good to all,
And his tender mercies are over all his works.
10 All thy works praise thee, O Lord !
And thy pious servants do bless thee.

*In the original, this psalm is an acrostic ; the successive verses beginning with the successive letters of the Hebrew alphabet.

11 They speak of the glory of thy kingdom,
And talk of thy power.
12 To make known to the sons of men his mighty deeds,
And the glorious majesty of his kingdom.
13 Thy kingdom is an everlasting kingdom,
And thy dominion endureth throughout all generations !

14 The LORD upholdeth all that fall,
And raiseth up all those that he bowed down.
15 The eyes of all wait upon thee ;
And thou givest them their food in due season.
16 Thou openest thine hand,
And satisfiest the desire of every living being.
17 The LORD is righteous in all his ways,
And gracious in all his works.
18 The LORD is nigh unto all them that call upon him,
To all that call upon him in truth.
19 He will fulfill the desire of them that fear him ;
He also will hear their cry, and will save them.
20 The LORD preserveth all them that love him ;
But all the wicked will he destroy.
21 My mouth shall speak the praise of the LORD ;
And let all flesh bless his holy name for ever and ever !

63. *PSALM CXLVI.*

*Exhortation to confidence in God alone, who is the creator of the universe,
the protector of the defenseless, and the eternal ruler.*

1 Hallelujah !
Praise the LORD, O my soul !
2 While I live will I praise the LORD ;
I will sing praises unto my God while I have my being.
3 Put not your trust in princes,
Nor in the son of man, in whom there is no help.
4 His breath goeth forth, he returneth to his earth ;
In that very day his plans perish.

5 Happy is he that hath the God of Jacob for his help,
   Whose hope is in the Lord his God:
6 Who made heaven and earth,
   The sea, and all that is therein;
   Who keepeth truth for ever:
7 Who executeth judgment for the oppressed;
   Who giveth food to the hungry:
   The Lord setteth free the prisoners;
8 The Lord openeth the eyes of the blind;
   The Lord raiseth up them that are bowed down;
   The Lord loveth the righteous;
9 The Lord preserveth the strangers;
   He upholdeth the fatherless and widow;
   But the way of the wicked he maketh crooked.

10 The Lord shall reign for ever,
   Thy God, O Zion, unto all generations!
   Hallelujah!

64. *PSALM CXLVII.*

Praising God, the Lord of nature, the upholder of all creatures, and especially the protector and benefactor of Israel.

1 Hallelujah!
   For it is good to sing praises unto our God;
   For it is pleasant, and praise is becoming.
2 The Lord buildeth up Jerusalem;
   He gathereth together the dispersed of Israel.
3 He healeth the broken in heart,
   And bindeth up their wounds.
4 He counteth the number of the stars;
   He calleth them all by names.
5 Great is our Lord, and mighty in power;
   His understanding is infinite.
6 The Lord upholdeth the meek;
   He bringeth the wicked down to the **ground.**

7 Sing unto the Lord with thanksgiving;
   Sing praises upon the harp unto our God !
8 Who covereth the heaven with clouds,
   Who prepareth rain for the earth,
   Who maketh grass to grow upon the mountains.
9 He giveth to the beast its food,
   And to the young ravens, which cry.
10 He delighteth not in the strength of the horse,
   He taketh no pleasure in the legs of a man.
11 The Lord taketh pleasure in them that fear him,
   In those that hope in his mercy.

12 Praise the Lord, O Jerusalem !
   Praise thy God, O Zion !
13 For he hath strengthened the bars of thy gates;
   He hath blessed thy children within thee.
14 He maketh peace in thy borders;
   He satisfieth thee with the finest of the wheat.
15 He sendeth forth his command to the earth;
   His word runneth very swiftly.
16 He giveth snow like wool;
   He scattereth the hoar-frost like ashes.
17 He casteth forth his ice like morsels;
   Who can stand before his cold ?
18 He sendeth out his word, and melteth them;
   He causes his wind to blow, and the waters flow.
19 He proclaimeth his word to Jacob,
   His statutes and his ordinances to Israel.
20 He hath not dealt so with any other nation;
   And as for his ordinances, they have not known them.
   Hallelujah !

65. *PSALM CXLVIII.*

All heavenly and earthly creatures, especially all human beings, are called upon to praise God.

1 Hallelujah !
   Praise ye the Lord from the heavens !

Praise him in the heights!
2 Praise ye him, all his angels!
Praise ye him, all his hosts!
3 Praise ye him, sun and moon!
Praise him, all ye stars of light!
4 Praise him, ye heavens of heavens!
And ye waters that are above the heavens!
5 Let them praise the name of the LORD;
For he commanded, and they were created.
6 He hath also established them for ever and ever;
He hath given them a law which shall not pass away.

7 Praise the LORD from the earth,
Ye sea-monsters, and all deeps!
8 Fire and hail, snow and vapor;
Thou stormy wind. that fulfillest his word!
9 Yea, mountains, and all hills!
Fruit trees, and all cedars!
10 Ye wild beasts, and all cattle!
Ye creeping things, and winged birds!
11 Ye kings of the earth, and all peoples,
Princes and all judges of the earth!
12 Both young men and maidens;
Old men and children!
13 Let them praise the name of the LORD,
For his name alone is exalted;
His glory is above the earth and heavens;
14 He exalteth the horn of his people,
The praise of all his pious servants,
Even of the children of Israel, a people near unto him.
Hallelujah!

66. *PSALM CL.*

Exhortation to praise God with all kinds of instruments.

1 Hallelujah!
Praise God in his sanctuary!

Praise him in his glorious firmament !
2 Praise him for his mighty deeds !
Praise him according to his excellent greatness !
3 Praise him with the sound of the trumpet !
Praise him with the psaltry and harp !
4 Praise him with the timbrel and dance !
Praise him with stringed instruments and the pipe !
5 Praise him upon the loud cymbals !
Praise him upon the high-sounding cymbals !
6 Let everything that hath breath praise the Lord !
Hallelujah !

The End.